CW00733973

Cliff Mogg was born in 1936 in Hazelbury Bryan, Dorset, but lived in Sherborne until being called up for National Service in the RAF. His father, Jack Mogg, was a well-known trade union and political activist. The family lived in a council estate to the north of the town and Cliff attended the Simons Road (Council) School and Foster's Boys' Grammar School. He has a younger brother, John. Cliff first entered journalism as an apprentice compositor with *The Western Gazette* in Yeovil. He later joined a weekly newspaper in Surrey, and has worked as a district chief reporter for daily newspapers in Hampshire and Berkshire. He is now a freelance journalist, and this is his second book. He lives in a small village near Basingstoke and he and his wife Jenny have four grown-up sons.

Following page
The author aged nine

The
COUNCIL HOUSE KID

Growing up in 1950s Sherborne

CLIFF MOGG

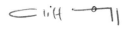

THE DOVECOTE PRESS

First published in 2000 by The Dovecote Press Ltd
Stanbridge, Wimborne, Dorset BH21 4JD

ISBN 1 874336 82 2

Designed and produced by The Dovecote Press Ltd
Printed and bound by the Baskerville Press, Salisbury

A CIP catalogue record of this book is
available from the British Library

1 3 5 7 9 8 6 4 2

Contents

I
Looking Back

I grew up in the small Dorset town of Sherborne during the days when people smoked Craven A, milk bottles had cardboard tops with a hole in the middle, and the jitterbug was everyone's favourite dance.

There were so few cars that I could play football in the road. Boys from the town's public school walked through the streets wearing straw boaters, and audiences rushed from the Carlton Picture Palace to avoid standing to attention for the National Anthem.

I was a youngster during the Second World War and early peacetime years when, on the radio, Dick Barton was a special agent and Donald Peers sang 'By a Babbling Brook'.

Television sets were almost a luxury, and those who had them watched 'Muffin the Mule' and 'Juke Box Jury' in black and white.

It was a time when summers were always sunny (I know they weren't, but it seems like that), and assistants stood behind grocery shop counters and greeted customers with a smile (that's probably my imagination running riot as well).

My home was in a large flat in the centre of Cheap Street, the main shopping street, and later a council estate in the north of the town. I lived there with my mum, dad and younger brother John.

It was in this small country town of 6,000 or so souls, with its Abbey, two castles (one a ruin), two public schools, and goodness knows how many pubs, that I learned to kick a ball, down a pint or two and discovered that girls had minds of their own.

The town's historic buildings, so beloved by today's tourists and television programme makers, were simply a backdrop to my rites of passage.

I attended the red brick Council School in Simons Road, which is still standing, and Foster's boys' grammar school, which isn't. I played football for Sherborne North End, sweat buckets playing table tennis at the Wessex Club in Westbury, and spent many an hour battling it out on the red shale tennis courts on The Terrace playing field.

Sherborne may have been a touch sleepy for some people, but not for me. My late father, Jack Mogg, was an outspoken left-wing trade unionist in a Tory town, and he enjoyed every minute of it.

Our home was a hotbed of working class politics, and I learnt the words of the Red Flag – 'the people's flag is deepest red' etc - long before those of the National Anthem.

The Communist *Daily Worker* (which later became *The Morning Star*) dropped through the letterbox every day, and the bookcase contained tomes by Aneurin Bevan, architect of the health service, and Harry Pollitt, a leading Communist.

These were the Cold War days, when America and Russia were at loggerheads, and those with left-wing leanings were viewed with suspicion by the police.

While dad argued against capitalism with anyone who would listen, I lived in fear of the two superpowers lighting the blue nuclear touch paper and sending us into oblivion.

During general and local elections our front room became Labour's campaign headquarters, and at other times it served as an 'office' for the local branch of the Transport and General Workers' Union.

After leaving school I joined *The Western Gazette* at Yeovil as an apprentice printer, and got an earbashing from a crusty old printer on my first day for spelling abattoir with two 'b's'. I told him I could spell 'slaughterhouse' which didn't impress him, and my apprenticeship took a rocky path from that day on.

I did my two years' National Service in the RAF. During my early training (called square bashing) I almost shot a corporal on the rifle range and that, not surprisingly, was the last time I touched a gun.

On returning home I had three clerical jobs, one with a tile flooring company, another with a printing company run by two warring brothers, and the other with a glove company where the boss breathed whisky fumes over me all day.

Forty or so years have elapsed since I caught a train to a new life as a newspaper reporter in Surrey. I visit Sherborne about once a year. It's where my roots are, and I still have fond memories of growing up in the place.

2

My Kind of Town

Sherborne in the 1940s and '50s was a town full of family run shops selling all manner of goods.

Among them were Ansty's sweetshop, Dickers' the greengrocers, Coakers' furniture shop, Everetts' the chemists, Freeman's sports shop, Caswell the fishmonger, and Coombes bakery with its upstairs restaurant.

Most of the shops were in Cheap Street, starting with Ansty's at the top and Everetts' at the bottom. Ansty's was owned by Eddie Ansty, a man of ample girth and little breath who enjoyed a snooze in a room at the back of the shop.

His visits to dreamland allowed youngsters to sneak into his shop, help themselves to his gobstoppers, and be away before he had even got out of his chair.

Not far from Eddie's shop was Curtis the hairdressers where young men could get a short back and sides and a packet of condoms from a discreet barber called Les.

Alongside was Hunt's Dairies which clanged to the sound of milk churns being rolled through the yard, and next door was Mould and Edwards, a delicatessen popular with the county set. Mr Mould, I believe, was a bald headed man who operated the bacon slicer with some dexterity. Mr Edwards had plastered down hair, a pencil thin moustache and a brisk manner.

The Dodge family sold antiques, and Lowmans menswear shop was managed by Ken Chant who played the sousaphone, a large brass instrument which produces single low notes, in the Yeo River Jazz Band.

Farther down stood Parsons' butcher's shop where Mr Baker, round-faced and bald-headed, attacked joints of meat with a cleaver as though his life depended on it.

His shop was next door to a slaughterhouse so customers knew his meat was fresh, but the squeals of protest from the cattle as they were herded up the adjoining passageway was slightly offputting.

Almost opposite was Freeman's which sold sports goods to the public schools. The shop, with its distinctive sign of two cricket bats and a ball, was one of two below the flat where I spent my early years. On the other side of our front door was a confectioners run by the Howe sisters.

Alongside Freeman's was Bakers where my Aunty Lot, down from London to escape the Blitz, worked selling bread and cakes which were made in the bakehouse at the back. The low ceiling shop also had a restaurant which was packed on market days with shoppers and farmers.

There were three greengrocers in the street. Dicker's and Glovers at the top and Burdens at the bottom. Mr and Mrs Dicker had a daughter called Monica, and the Glovers had two sons called Bill and Bob.

Down the road from Dicker's was a dental surgery where the sight of instruments being sterilised in pans of boiling water put me off dentists for life. I kicked up such a commotion on my first visit that those in the waiting room looked at each other and wondered if they really needed to see the dentist after all.

Of the other traders in Cheap Street, Everetts' chemist shop did its best to provide a cure for most things. Those requiring medicine of a different type could nip into an off-licence next door where they would be served by 'Butch'

Harvey, who played right back for Sherborne's football team.

Mr and Mrs Gillard owned a tobacconist and men's hairdressers near the entrance to the Methodist Church, Eldridge and Pope's off-licence was managed by Joe Shambler who always wore a bow tie, and Bird's womenswear shop was run by the gentlemanly Dickie Bird who played tennis in long trousers. Opposite was Dyers, which sold bikes on the ground floor and toys on the floor above.

Upstairs in the Abbey Bookshop the gnome-like Bertie Chamberlain smoked a pipe, was happiness personified, and spent his days printing wedding invitations, headed notepaper and posters for dances and similar events.

Minterne's, which stood on the corner of Abbey Road, was an early version of a do-it-yourself shop, and the Three Wishes restaurant was popular with little old ladies.

Round the corner in Long Street, Harry Hunt and his brother David cheerfully sold toys to children and air pistols and lethal looking knives to a slightly older age group, and out the back cheerful Reg Roberts was kept busy mending bicycles.

On the other side of the road was Spiller's hardware shop owned by 'Skip' Spiller, the local scoutmaster. Child's garage was nearby.

Macnallys' newsagent's shop in Church Lane was managed by burly Bob White who, during the summer months, trundled up to the wicket as a fairly fast bowler for the town's cricket team.

Pedley and White men's outfitters stood in Half Moon Street, next door to Isaacs' hairdressers. Opposite was the House of Steps restaurant, and Phillips and Handover, the town's only department store, was a short distance away.

Bretts' seed merchants faced the Abbey, and round the corner in Digby Road was Reeves, a draughty shed-like furniture shop where tables, chairs and other items were displayed on a cold concrete floor.   The salesman was a short man in a grey smock who wore two pairs of socks to keep his feet warm.

Not far away was the railway station where one of my mates, Tony Sprague, sold newspapers and magazines from a hut on the platform. He kept some magazines hidden under the counter, and very interesting they were too.

Liptons, the International Stores and the Co-op, which all sold groceries, seemed like intruders among the town's family owned shops. As did Woolworths which boasted that it never sold anything priced more than sixpence (two-and-a-half pence in today's money).

The Co-op. whose manager was Mr Gosney, didn't have cash tills. Instead the money winged its away in canisters, attached to overhead wires, between the counters and a cashier at the end of the store.

Eating out in the evening was limited to two fish and chip shops. Samways was at the top of George Street and the other, run by Jock Quirk, was in Westbury.

The shop windows were cleaned by a tall thin man nicknamed 'Dewdrop', whose runny nose caused him problems when he was perched on his ladder. It could also cause problems for people who walked under his ladder without an umbrella.

3
The Wartime Years

In the week that I was born Hitler opened the first Volkswagon factory in Saxony. His aim, apparently, was to do for Germany what Henry Ford had done for the United States and put the nation 'on wheels'.

That was in February 1936. As everyone knows, he soon lost interest in car building and decided to start a war instead, with the result that he almost brought a premature end to my life.

We thought we were safe in Sherborne, a speck on the map which surely wouldn't interest the one-time Austrian born painter turned warmonger. How wrong we were.

I was four-years-old when the Luftwaffe dropped a stack of bombs on the town, including a few which exploded almost on our doorstep.

The raid happened sixty years ago, but the memory of that Monday in September 1940 is still crystal clear. We were living in the Tonmore House flat, and minutes before the 387 bombs fell I was in the garden, playing with a tennis ball and dreaming of becoming the world's greatest footballer (an ambition, which like many others, remained unfulfilled).

As I listened to the German bombers droning overhead, mum called out 'Clifford, get indoors now.' For once I didn't argue and reached the downstairs passageway just as the bombs started to fall.

The shockwaves reverberated through the building.

Mum and I, and Miss Freeman from the sports shop, who had joined us in the downstairs hallway, seemed to spin through mid air. I was sent into orbit and landed in the arms of the voluptuous 'Girlie' Freeman who clutched me to her bosom. The earth moved in a big way for me that day, although of course not in the modern sense of the expression.

Across the open air passageway the terrified Howe sisters cowered beneath a table as the bombs rocked the town, sending their jars of sweets crashing to the shop floor. I can't remember if their hair, which was tied in buns, was grey before the raid. It certainly was afterwards.

Eighteen people were killed and 32 injured in what was the first German bombing raid on a West Country town in the Second World War. Later it transpired that Sherborne had not been on Hitler's hit-list. The Luftwaffe were making for the Westland Aircraft Company factory in Yeovil, but they were spotted by RAF fighters and mistakenly dropped their bombs on Sherborne when a break in the cloud revealed a town of about the same size and in about the same place as Yeovil.

Dad arrived home from his job at the Fleet Air Arm station at Zigwells, a few miles to the north of Sherborne, where he worked as a civilian driver, to see a pall of smoke and debris dust hanging over the town. He drove his lorry to the outskirts and walked in, convinced that he would find us and Tonmore House obliterated.

Relieved to discover that we had survived, he decided it was high time we had an air raid shelter to dive into should Jerry pay a return visit. He didn't enjoy gardening, so digging a 10ft deep hole was a superhuman effort on his part.

He spent hours hacking away with a shovel and a

pickaxe, the sweat trickling into his eyes. From the depths of the hole he could be heard muttering and swearing in a sort of metronomic rhythm. Each crash of the pickaxe would be followed by a verbal assault on Hitler: Crash, 'that **** Hitler'. . . bang 'that **** Hitler'. And so it went on until he was satisfied the hole was big enough for us to fit into.

Once the excavation was finished, he conjured up some wooden planks to shore up the walls. He used corrugated iron sheets for the roof which he covered with dirt to try to make sure the Germans wouldn't see it if they flew over. The camouflaged shelter wouldn't have won any design awards, but dad was rightly proud of it.

Several times we dived in there, wearing coats over our nightclothes, as the air raid siren wailed across the town where blackout curtains hung in every home. The alert was usually caused by German bombers flying over to attack the Westlands' aircraft factory.

Mum, I and uncles and aunts who were living with us, would sit shivering in the dank and musty shelter, while dad stood outside and gave us a running commentary on the raid - 'Oh, something in Yeovil's been hit...I don't like the look of that...hey, that was a big one.' He didn't even bother to wear his tin helmet – supplied for his duties as an Air Raid warden - which mum thought was a trifle reckless.

Survival was the name of the game during the war, not just when the German planes flew overhead, but at mealtimes as well. With sugar and other basic foodstuffs rationed, mum's culinary skills were tested to the limit.

Her powdered egg omelettes were delicious. Helpings of spam and corned beef, both out of a tin, were also tolerable, as was powdered potato. But my stomach couldn't cope with egg custard, a gunge which slithered down my throat – and made an equally rapid attempt to come up again. Junket was another pudding which had the same disturbing effect on my digestive system. I couldn't face it, despite being told by mum that, like all disgusting food, 'it's good for you, so eat it up.'

Rice pudding also appeared regularly on the dinner table. Too regularly for my liking. It was put in front of me so often that the rice pickers in the paddy fields must have worked overtime to meet the demand.

Away from the meal table mum gave me Syrup of Figs to keep me regular, and an awful concoction of milk and a raw egg if I seemed in need of a tonic.

Mum really came into her own at Christmas. The wash-house was in a building alongside the open air passageway leading from Tonmore House to the garden. It was there that she filled the large stone boiler with water, lit the wood fire underneath, and then cooked the Christmas puddings by immersing them in the water.

The puddings were in earthenware basins with a cloth tied over the top, and they soon disappeared in the steam which billowed out of the wash-house. The building looked for all the world as though it was on fire, and it's a wonder no-one ever called the fire brigade.

Those puddings tasted delicious. I was really lucky as well because I always found myself eating the piece with the sixpence in it on Christmas Day!

Tonmore House was a large two-storey flat, and during the war years it was like Waterloo Station, full of people, including two uncles, three aunties and a cousin who moved in with us from London and Portsmouth to escape the Blitz.

Evenings were even more congested when sailors from nearby Zigwells and Zeals Fleet Air Arm stations, where dad worked during the war, popped in for a chat, a cup of tea and extremely long games of chess. The board was often put away, the pieces in place, so that the game could be continued on another evening.

The sailors were a friendly but competitive lot, as I soon discovered. They showed no mercy when they played me at draughts, allowing me one or two moves at most before wiping me off the board. I soon decided there were more interesting ways of spending my time, and made a beeline for the attic whenever they came through the front door. And that's where I stayed, out of sight and playing with my toys and reading the Beano and other comics until it was time for bed.

Along with egg custard and being humiliated at draughts, another wartime horror were visits by dad's mother, grandma Rider, who remarried after her first husband had been killed in the First World War. She was a fearsome looking woman who had lost an eye and didn't have a glass one as a replacement. She wore spectacles with a frosted lens to cover the hole.

Naturally she didn't sleep with her spectacles on, so I dreaded her calling me into her bedroom in the morning.

'Clifford, come in and say hello to grandma,' she'd say.

'Oh no,' I'd groan, as I opened the door to find her looking at me with her one good eye. The sight of the cavernous gap where the other eye should have been was just too much for my tender years, and I would leave the room in double quick time.

Another feature of grandma Rider's visits was her insistence on eating tripe and onions. A distinctly unappetising dish in view of the fact that tripe is nothing more than cow's intestines. Mum did her best to avoid cooking it, but inevitably the call would come from the lounge, 'Stella, I'd love tripe and onions for dinner today.' Mum would grimace and try to keep her stomach under control as she stood over the gas stove preparing the awful concoction. Dinner was never an enjoyable occasion at those times. Eating our sausages and mash was extremely difficult with grandma Rider sitting on the other side of the table slurping down her cow's intestines and onions.

Grandma Rider died while cleaning a door knocker at her Winchester home. As far as I know eating tripe wasn't the cause of her death, although it could well have been a contributory factor.

It's strange what people used to eat in those days. My uncle Stan couldn't wait to get his teeth into rabbit's brains, and there was nothing grandad Watts - mum's dad - liked more than a hunk of blue cheese with maggots crawling out of it.

'It's really mature when you can see the maggots,' he would tell me.

'Yes grandad, I quite believe it,' I'd reply, desperately hoping that he wouldn't offer me a piece. The thought of maggots wriggling around in my stomach was more than I could bear.

More to my taste was the candy and chewing gum handed out by the American servicemen based in Sherborne during the war. Juicy Fruit chewing gum was a favourite. Food rationing meant that we could buy only a handful of sweets each week, apart from those we obtained illegally from Eddie Ansty, so the GI's supplies were more than welcome. Americans have never been more popular than they were in those days.

It was during this period that a visit to the Carlton Picture Palace put me off broad beans for life. The film was 'Phantom of the Opera', a horror epic and light years away from Andrew Lloyd Webber's musical version.

I was about nine-years-old at the time, and the sight of the Phantom's face being burnt away with acid had me sliding down the cinema seat and on to the floor. When I arrived home mum served up meat, potatoes and broad beans for dinner. I tucked into it, but that night the Phantom came back to haunt me. I had the mother and father of nightmares as he chased me through the cellars of the Paris Opera House.

That was the end of eating broad beans for me. They are forever associated with that Phantom nightmare, and I haven't eaten them since.

For the life of me, I still can't understand why I was allowed to watch the film. Not only did it put me off broad beans, it put me off opera as well.

4
Countryside Trips

Most of my holidays in the post-war years were spent visiting Gran and Grandad Watts about 14 miles away at Hazelbury Bryan, a village which lies in the shadow of Bulbarrow Hill in the heart of Dorset.

Sometimes I cycled to see them, puffing my way up Sherborne Hill, through Alweston and Holwell, over the King Stag crossroads and into Hazelbury Bryan. On other occasions I caught the market day bus in Digby Road and travelled in relative comfort.

Gran and Grandad lived in a tiny stone-built end-of-terrace cottage without any mod cons. They boiled the kettle in the fire place and cooked their food on a tiny oil stove in an outhouse-cum-kitchen at the back.

Going to the loo meant a trek up the garden to the 'thunder box' - a draughty wooden building, similar to a night-watchman's hut, where I was convinced rats prowled in the long grass outside.

With torn up sheets of newspaper serving as toilet paper, I would sit there with one eye looking out for rats and the other devouring the news of the past few days. I never actually saw a rat, but I often heard some disturbing rustling noises outside.

There were no flushing facilities, and grandad would bury the contents of the bucket in the garden, which probably explained why he had such a magnificent crop of potatoes and other vegetables. The cabbages and brussel sprouts were extremely green, and the potatoes had a flavour all of their own. As for his runner beans, they grew to untold heights.

Thankfully it wasn't necessary to sally up the garden at night if I was taken short. Gran and Grandad thoughtfully provided a chamber pot – or po as it was generally known – for such emergencies. It was kept under the bed with a cloth over it. Hygiene wasn't too high on the agenda, but everyone seemed to survive.

When darkness fell we would sit and talk, or read, in the glow of an oil lamp. There were also times when we would listen to the radio, made of Bakelite and powered by a large glass accumulator battery which stood alongside it.

It was during one of my holidays with them that I listened to my first Cup Final on the radio. Through the atmospheric crackle I could just about hear Raymond Glendenning commentating on the match between Charlton Athletic and Burnley.

The oil lamp wasn't the only thing which glowed as we sat in the tiny living room. My insides also felt on fire from the brandy which gran slipped into my cups of tea as well as hers. 'Have a drop of this, it'll do you good', she'd say, and who was I to argue. I certainly preferred it to junket and egg custard.

Gran and Grandad, a powerfully-built man who spent his working days lifting huge sacks of corn at the local mill, were typical of their time. Apart from the occasional trips to Sherborne and Sturminster Newton on the market-day bus, they rarely stepped outside the village.

With egg-laying chickens at the bottom of the garden, and vegetables in regular supply, they were almost self-sufficient. A baker called once a week, they got their milk from a local farm, groceries from the village shop, and

Uncle Alec, who lived nearby, supplied them with rabbits which he shot in fields at the back of his house.

Their water supply was from an outside butt which collected the rain. With no bathroom, the only way of staying clean was to squat in a tin bath which had a microscopic amount of hot water at the bottom.

Talk about a Spartan lifestyle, they took their baths in a cold and draughty outhouse which was just as uncomfortable as the 'Thunder Box'. As I stood in the bath, my goose-pimpled body turning blue, Gran would say: 'Wash what's possible from the top . . . wash what's possible from the bottom . . . and then wash the possible.' Whatever did she mean?

Living with Gran and Grandad was Aunty Flo, one of mum's four sisters. By day she worked as a conductor on the Bere Regis buses, and at week-ends she looked after the village hall, which was almost opposite the cottage.

One Saturday evening I accompanied Aunty Flo to the corrugated iron hall where she intended locking up after a dance. As we walked through the door we were greeted, not by the sight of dancers locked in a last minute embrace, but by a gang of gipsies locked in combat with soldiers from a nearby army camp.

The band, deciding that in the circumstances there was no need to play the 'Last Waltz', had long since disappeared from the stage as the gipsies attacked the army's finest with studded belts. The village lads were nowhere to be seen either, although some of the soldiers' girlfriends were screaming at them from the stage.

Aunty Flo, shocked that a genteel village dance could end in such mayhem, ushered me out of the hall and decided to let the warring parties fight to a finish. She didn't find any bodies in the hall the next morning, although it took her some time to clean the blood spattered floor.

Back in Sherborne I was packed off once a week to attend the Cubs, and later the Scouts, who met in a wooden hut in the bottom corner of Hound Street field. I can't say I was a wholehearted member of either organisation. Sitting in front of a camp fire singing songs like 'Ging Gang Gooly', and trying unsuccessfully to tie a variety of complicated knots, was a pretty uninspiring way to spend an evening as far as I was concerned.

I just about mastered the reef knot, but the sheepshank totally defeated me. As for attempting to light a fire by rubbing two sticks together, I soon decided that it was an impossible task and that Baden Powell had dreamed it up because he had run out of ideas to occupy our time. Hadn't he ever heard of matches?

It was this general air of apathy which probably persuaded Cyril Ransome, one of the Scout leaders, to entertain us by trying to electrocute himself. The hut was surrounded by an electrified wire fence, powered by a battery, and Cyril's party piece was to put his tongue on the wire and leap in the air as the shock passed through his body.

We always expected to see him expire with sparks shooting out of his head, but the voltage was low enough to allow him to walk away cackling and unscathed. The more imaginatively inclined among us often thought of connecting the wire to the mains electricity, thereby giving Cyril the sort of shock which would have sent him soaring towards the stars, but wiser heads prevailed.

When I arrived home mum would always ask: 'Did you have an interesting time at Scouts?' As much as I was tempted, I could never bring myself to reply: 'Same as usual really, Cyril showed us how to electrocute ourselves . . .'. I don't think she would have been too impressed.

During this period my sister Jean, who was John's twin, died from gastroenteritis when only nine months old. Her death was an extremely sad interlude in my happy childhood. I was ten at the time, and can still remember how devastated my parents were when she passed away.

Jean is buried in Sherborne cemetery, but I didn't attend the funeral. Dad, whose approach to life was always unconventional, spared me the upset by sending me off to The Terrace to play in a football match.

Hound Street field, where sheep markets were held during the week, was also the place where a group of us, Johnny Crane, Bobby Davis, John Curtis, and one or two others played endless games of football, often in ankle deep, sticky mud.

We used our coats and jumpers as goalposts, and played with a leather football which was like a lump of lead when wet. The football had an inner tube which always needed repairing, and a lace which stuck out and turned heading into an act of bravery. Making contact with it would leave us with a stinging forehead, watering eyes and an awful headache.

The one day on which we didn't play football was Sunday, the most mind numbingly boring day of the week. In common with most other children, I wasn't allowed out to play.

Instead I was sent off to the Methodist Sunday school by mum where Miss Chubb's patience was tested to the limit as she tried to interest me in stories from the Bible. She failed. Her readings of Moses in the bullrushes and similar Biblical tales were pretty tame stuff compared to the adventures of Enid Blyton's 'Famous Five' and the 'Just William' stories. My later attendance at Coombe church was pretty short-lived. I and a few of the Sunday morning rear pew regulars soon started sneaking off to The Terrace playing field in our best suits to mess around with a tennis ball. We were glad to get away and the vicar was glad to see us go. He had long since decided that trying to save our souls was a lost cause.

It was during one of our Sunday morning visits to The Terrace that someone threw a ball in the air and shouted 'head it' to Tony Sprague. He did – and collapsed on the ground in agony. Showing the same sense of humour which almost led to the electrocution of Cyril Ransome, the perpetrator (no, it wasn't me) had lobbed a rock hard cricket ball in the air instead of the expected tennis ball. It left Tony with the difficult task of explaining to his parents how a visit to church had left him with glazed eyes and an egg size lump on his head. I believe he tried to pass it off as an act of God.

A smiling me with Grandma Rider. It was a different story in later life – I used to hide whenever she was around.

I keep a firm grip on our dog Nell as grandad Watts looks on in the garden of his cottage in Hazelbury Bryan. I was about five at the time.

Above: Simons Road (Council) School on board the *Queen Elizabeth* during a summer camp day trip to Southampton in 1946. I am peering over the lifebelt. Standing to the right, in the back row, is our no-nonsense teacher, Jack Read.

Opposite top: Foster's School in Tinney's Lane, which I attended from 1947 to 1952. The building was demolished in 1992 following a decision to end grammar school education in the town (photo, Sherborne Museum).

Opposite bottom: The Carlton Picture Palace in Newland which closed in the late 1960s. Sadly, the building, with all its silver-screen memories, was bulldozed in 1989 to make way for the Somerfields car park (photo, Sherborne Museum).

Receiving my Blackmore Vale cup winner's medal at Templecombe. Waiting behind me is one of my Sherborne North End team-mates, Ernie 'Wacker' Male, a more than useful goal scorer.

5
Schooldays

My time at Sherborne Council School was a mixture of classroom success and playground scrapes, the worst of which landed me in hospital after tripping over and cutting my head. On my return several days later my teacher, Mrs F. Holdway, wrote to my parents saying she was glad my forehead had healed so well. 'It was a nasty bump, wasn't it,' she wrote. My recollection is that it was more than a nasty bump, but it's a bit late to start arguing with Mrs Holdway's prognosis. All I will say is that I bear the scar to this day.

The teachers at Council School were a stern bunch, none more so than Jack Read, a blunt talking northerner who kept an iron grip on the class. 'Are you paying attention,' he would bellow at anyone who showed the slightest sign of letting their concentration waver. It was no good pretending you had been hanging on his every word, either, because in a voice which bore a remarkable resemblance to Fred Trueman's, but with a higher decibel rating, he would say: 'Come to the front and repeat what I've been saying.'

If he picked on me, then I knew I was in really big trouble. Not only did I get a classroom rollicking, but I also lived in fear of a second ticking off at home because Jack and dad were close friends. Living under that sort of threat probably helped my concentration, but it did nothing for my nervous disposition.

To the relief, I'm sure, of the headmaster, Mr Care, dramatic events were few and far between at Council School. There was one occasion, however, when a game of rounders came to an abrupt end after the bat slipped out of a boy's hand as he swiped at the ball. The bat missed the ball and connected with another boy's head, leaving him covered in blood and needing hospital treatment. Mr Care put the rounder's bat in a cupboard and that was the last we saw of it.

When I was seven-years-old my parents received another letter from Miss Holdway – who apologised for the 'scratchy school pen' used to write the note – which sparked hopes (totally false, as it turned out) that they had spawned a son for whom academic success beckoned.

She wrote: 'Mr Care was so pleased with Clifford's work when there was an informal exam last week that, as a result, he will move up to Miss Crocker's class next term a year before he need, which is rather an achievement for a little boy of his age.'

I've asked myself many times since, where did it all go wrong? I seemed to get stuck on the lower rungs of the scholastic ladder after passing the eleven plus for a place at Foster's Boys' Grammar School in the town.

Life was plain sailing at the Council School where the teachers regularly wrote on my reports 'a very good term's work', or 'Clifford has made good progress in all subjects.' Handing over those reports to mum and dad was never a problem.

When I arrived home with my Foster's School reports, I would put the sealed envelope on the table and quickly disappear, allowing time for my father's temper to simmer down after the first reading.

Apart from one successful spell when I gained third place

in the overall exam results, my reports indicated a certain lack of rapport with the teachers.

In 1950 my form master wrote on my report: 'His progress is very slow. He should concentrate a little more on his work.' Fair enough, but I have to say that he didn't seem totally focussed when he taught us divinity, as it was known in those days. He seemed as bored as the rest of us with the subject.

Sitting behind his desk at the head of the class, he would tell us to open the Bible at Corinthians, or whatever, and leave us to study certain passages. Initially we would stare silently at the page knowing full well that, within five minutes he would be sound asleep. A short portly man with a bald head, he would slumber with his chin resting on his chest while we got on with a pencil and paper game of battleships or hangman.

He would set extremely easy exam questions in the hope that the relaxed nature of his divinity lessons wouldn't show through in the results. It probably explains why someone like myself, who had only a limited knowledge of the Bible (well, hardly any knowledge at all, to be honest), managed to come fourth out of twenty-three in one exam. The result was as big a shock to dad as it was to me. As an atheist, he was extremely relieved when I told him that the exam result was a fluke, and that I had no interest in becoming a priest.

Maths lessons under the stockily built 'Micky' Miller were a totally different, and unnerving, experience. He took the subject very seriously indeed and seemed convinced that everyone was capable of becoming an Albert Einstein. Faced with a mathematical dunderhead like me, he would try to explain the complexities of algebra and geometry by catching hold of the small hairs on my neck and pushing my face on to the desk.

As my nose became more squashed by the second, he would ask: 'x plus y equals what...?' and then wait for the answer which never came. He used the same method to try to imprint the Pythagoras' theorem on my brain. My voice muffled by the close proximity of the desk, I would mumble: 'The square on the hypotenuse of a right-angle triangle is equal to the sum of the squares on the other two sides.' All very impressive until Mr Miller asked me what it meant. Repeating it parrot fashion was one thing, explaining it was another. I didn't have a clue what it meant then, and I still haven't.

Another master who seemed to believe that pain was the pathway to knowledge was Mr Wilkins, who taught woodwork. He soon worked out that my use of the wood plane and chisel left a lot to be desired. 'Standard of work low' he said in one report when I came 20 out of 24 in an exam. I don't know who was below me, but they must have been pretty awful.

Anyway, I might have fared better in Mr Wilkins' woodwork classes if my hands hadn't been trembling with fear. He would hurl a piece of wood at any pupil who failed to follow his instructions, and he did so with unerring accuracy. When Mr Wilkins bellowed 'pay attention, Mogg', I knew that within seconds an offcut would be whistling its way towards my head.

I don't know if Foster's School attracted eccentric teachers, but we seemed to have our fair share of them. An English teacher named 'Gobby' Gibling would balance pieces of chalk on his bald head and say, a trifle unnecessarily I felt, 'chalk on head'. I always thought it was a cue for men in white coats to walk in, but it was Gibling's unusual method of explaining the complexities of the

English language. We would sit there, willing the piece of chalk to roll off his head, but it never did.

For a couple of terms we were taught English by a master with one arm. With his armless jacket sleeve tucked in the pocket, he stood before us on his first day and warned: 'If you upset me I will either hit you with my one remaining arm, or jump out of the window.' We must have been a bunch of cowards because no-one ever tested his novel threat. I would love to be able to say that I saw him launch himself head first through a window, yelling 'I've had enough' as he plummeted towards the playground, but quite honestly I can't.

There were some teachers, of course, who brought a touch of normality to the school. Stanley McKay, who taught history, was an urbane and civilised man, as was Mr Maltby whose relaxed style made art lessons a joy. His easy-going manner befitted someone who claimed – jokingly I'm sure— to have often found himself shooting at his own side more than the enemy during his time as an ack ack gunner in the war.

Our portly singing teacher, 'Daddy' Wearden, the Abbey organist and choir-master, was a kindly man who never gave up trying to cajole a group of reluctant boys to sing in tune. Along with the cooks, whose school dinners were mostly greeted with a time honoured chorus of moans, he had the most thankless task in the school and rarely, if ever, experienced a sense of achievement.

He spent several lessons valiantly trying to persuade us to sing Schubert's 'The Trout'. It was to no avail. One lad finally pleaded: 'We'd sooner go and catch one, sir,' but Mr Wearden didn't take the bait. I finally dropped out of his class at the age of 14. I know when it was because he wrote on my Easter report, with a bluntness which indicated he was glad to see the back of me: 'Voice breaking'.

For sheer torture, physical education in the gym took some beating. There were those in the class, Jack Wintersgill among them, who could swing from rope to rope before completing a triple somersault over the box (well, maybe one somersault) and landing on their feet. I've rarely landed on my feet during my journey through life, and I certainly didn't in the gym.

My failure to perform amazing feats of agility regularly incurred the wrath of Jimmy Bogan, the PE master whose brusque sergeant major manner was of no help to me whatsoever.

He expressed nothing but contempt as he watched me struggle to climb to the top of a rope suspended from the gym ceiling. 'Put some effort into it, boy,' he would shout. (Who did he think I was, Tarzan?). His exasperation was frightening to behold as I clambered over the box (no triple somersault for me) before crumpling in a heap on the other side. Hanging on the wallbars was a form of Chinese torture in my book, and my inability to do a handstand and backward roll simply confirmed what he already knew, that I was a miserable failure in the gym.

Amazing as it may seem, my relationship with the master who followed him was even more fractious. Arthur Critchley got it into his head that I was making fun of him. On one of my reports he wrote 'attitude not always co-operative'. He seemed to believe that, because I played football and cricket for the school first teams, I should have been able to act like a circus acrobat in the gym. How wrong could anyone be? Funnily enough, after leaving school we regularly played each other at tennis. Fair play to him, he took his defeats quite well.

Overseeing this rather eclectic example of the country's

teaching profession was the headmaster, 'Hubert' Lush, who had the eccentric habit of gardening by torchlight at night. He was the centre of an incident on the cricket field which provided me with an early lesson in the power of those with authority.

It happened during the annual first eleven's match against the staff. I was called upon to bowl my offbreaks against Mr Lush who was a batsman of limited strokes and even more limited footwork. Presumably everyone thought that my innocuous 'donkey drops' would provide him with an opportunity to hit at least a couple of runs.

So in I ran, over went my arm, and 'click' went the bails – joy of joys, I'd bowled the headmaster first ball. 'Owzat', I shouted, waiting for the rest of the team to crowd round and shake my hand. Then it dawned on me, I was the only one celebrating.

As 'old man' Lush stood his ground I saw our captain, Robert Earnshaw, replacing the bails and saying to the crestfallen headmaster: 'Stay there, sir, the wicketkeeper knocked the bails off accidently.'

I was about to say something like 'come off it, I bowled him fair and square', when I saw Robert, who had obviously received lessons in how to progress in life, put his fingers to his lips and then signal to me to continue bowling. He did very well at school, did Robert. Much better than me.

Come to think of it, my moments of glory on the sports field – rare as they were – never seemed to be greeted with any great enthusiasm. During a match against the old boys I took what was the best catch of my young life. I dived full stretch to get my hand under the ball, which was inches from the ground, and held on to it.

When players take catches like that in Test matches they

are surrounded by back slapping team-mates. When I stood up, proudly holding the ball aloft, I was immediately confronted by a 'Doubting Thomas' of an umpire in the shape of French master Ernest Hulme. Instead of congratulating me on a magnificent catch, he inquired: 'Are you sure you caught that? Didn't it hit the ground first?' He wasn't convinced and continued to mutter away as the batsman, casting disbelieving looks in my direction, reluctantly trudged from the field.

There was a similar negative response when I hit a quick fire 25 runs to get the team out of a hole in a match against the local police. As I strode back to the pavilion, feeling on top of the world, I was greeted by a stony faced 'Micky' Miller. 'That was a bit of a slog,' he grunted. 'That's not how we've taught you to bat.'

Each year there was a short period when the sound of sneezing and coughing would reverberate through the school. Boys with handkerchiefs clasped to their faces, or hobbling with knee or ankle 'injuries', would explain their sudden incapacity to an increasingly sceptical Jimmy Bogan. These were the pupils for whom the mere thought of running in the school cross country championship was too much to bear.

They were given marshalling duties on the day of the race to try to ensure none of us took short cuts along the route from the school gates in Tinney's Lane, along New Road, up through The Grove to the top of Sherborne Hill and back again.

I contented myself by running part of the course, and walking the rest. Along the way I would chat to like-minded souls (it made for a very congenial afternoon) and arrive back long after Jimmy Bogan had put his stopwatch away. There was no sign of the winner either. He had long since collected his prize and gone home.

Only one of my contemporaries, so far as I know, attained what might be called celebrity status, and that was Derek Boshier whose father ran the Britannia pub in the town. While the rest of class got on with painting vaguely recognisable pictures of houses, trees and people, Derek would seemingly spray paint in all directions. His paintings looked a multi-coloured mess, but he had obviously sussed out modern art at an early age and went on to gain international fame as a 'pop' artist with his imaginative use of cereal packets, drink cans and other everyday items.

He studied alongside David Hockney, a bespectacled artist of some repute, at the Royal College of Art. I once saw Derek on television taking part in a serious discussion about the art world, and my mind couldn't help flitting back to one of the school's Commoners' Concerts where Derek dressed up as a bird and sang 'I thought I saw a pussy cat creeping up on me'. As I listened to him chatting away in an authoritative voice, I couldn't help thinking that acting the fool at school doesn't necessarily mean that people won't take you seriously in later life.

Not that I escaped scot-free where embarrassing moments on stage were concerned. Ten of us were chosen to sing 'Green grow the rushes oh' in a school concert. I was delegated to sing 'I'll give you four oh. . .', which was a bit of serious miscasting on the part of Geoffrey 'Pansy' Hewitt, the master in charge of this particular item.

I was petrified of standing in front of the footlights, and couldn't stop myself swaying from side to side as sweat poured from my armpits and my legs turned to jelly. The sight of my nervous tic drove 'Pansy' to distraction. 'For goodness sake stay still when you sing,' he'd yell. But the more he bawled at me during rehearsals, the worse it became until I was nearly turning full circle. My solo part took about 45 seconds, but it seemed like 45 hours as I struggled to stop swaying, remember the words and keep in tune. My miserable performance before an audience of parents (I told mine not to come) convinced an exasperated 'Pansy' that I wasn't a natural footlighter, and he was more than happy to let me join the backstage staff for future concerts.

Each year at Foster's we would have a speech day where those who had paid attention in class received their prizes and the rest of us sat there bored and with aching backsides. There was always a speech by a member of the great and the good whose words of wisdom seldom had any impact.

The ceremony would end with the school song, which we sang with gusto because we knew we would soon be making our way home. With an amalgam of flat notes and breaking voices we would belt out:

'Thanks to Richard Foster's goodness,
Here we work and play.
Learning lessons that will help us,
This and ev'ry day . . .' – and so on.

On the stage music teacher Wearden, his face etched with pain as he listened to our assault on the school song, longed for a trap door to open up to rescue him from the awful racket. Standing alongside the special guest, headmaster Lush stared straight ahead wondering if a music teacher was perhaps surplus to the school's requirements, while Mr Maltby smiled broadly as he appeared to enjoy every second of our shambolic interpretation of Littleton C. Powys' words and J. Barham Johnson's music.

On my office wall, as I write, is a photograph of the whole school taken in 1949 – schoolchildren from a bygone era. Five rows of boys, most with their hair parted neatly on the left-hand side, wearing blazers and ties, some looking serious, some with cherubic smiles, and one looking sorry for himself because he is sporting the most marvellous black eye.

In the fourth row from the front is one of my contempories, Ken House, who became so attached to the school that he later returned to teach physical education and maths before being promoted to Headmaster. Not far away, in the next row down, is Alan Hicks, who rose to the dizzy rank of Air Commodore in the RAF, and on his right is Len Crane who became a professional footballer and played in goal for Portsmouth. Len's career path was reasonably predictable, Alan's less so, even though he was a stalwart member of the School Cadet Force.

Sitting in the middle of the front row, with their hands clasped or folded, are the masters – Messrs Wilkins, Bogan, Greenwood, Maltby, Miller, Lush, Welcher, Hulme, Hewitt, McKay and Palmer. Greenwood taught Latin, Palmer taught English, and 'Wasty' Welcher was the science master whose experiments with test tubes and bunsen burners often created awful smells, but failed to capture my interest.

In those days our parents had to sign a Dorset Education Authority contract pledging that we would attend the school 'regularly and punctually' and that we would observe 'all the rules and regulations' of the education authority and the school governors.

The contract also stated, in view of the money being spent by the authority on our education, that parents had to 'undertake and agree that the pupil shall not be withdrawn from the said school.' In other words, like it or lump it, we had to stay there until we were 16-years-old.

I left Foster's in 1952 with mixed feelings and with three

School Certificates in English Language, Literature and History, all at Ordinary (very ordinary, I'd say) Level.

My happiest times were on the sports field, playing football, cricket and tennis. Other than that, the place sort of passed me by. I hated wearing the brown and yellow cap and blazer (the cap came off as soon as I was out of the school gates), and I didn't appreciate going to school on Saturday mornings to make up for playing sport on Wednesday afternoons.

But worst of all, there were no girls to liven up the lessons. Girls who passed the 11-plus exam went to Lord Digby's School where they were kept in convent-like seclusion behind a 12ft high brick wall. Fraternising was frowned upon, although plenty of it went on after school hours.

Funnily enough, my abiding memory of Foster's is the smell of boiled cabbage which seemed to permanently waft from the kitchen and hang over the playground. Thank goodness I never had to eat the stuff.

6

Union Rebels

Our family has its roots in Dorset, with the first recorded ancestor being John Mogge who married Edyith Nele at Lydlinch in 1593. Some time in the 1600s we dropped the 'e' off the end of our surname, and that's the way it has stayed until this day.

Dad's branch of the family moved to Wells in Somerset in the 1800s and made their mark as successful business people, running a bakery and an agricultural machinery business in the city for many years.

One member of the family, Eric Mogg, was Mayor of Wells. In one newspaper cutting he was described as a 'modest man who never sought the headlines.' A typical Mogg I'd say!

I was born in the Dorset village of Hazelbury Bryan on 21 February 1936. Dad, who was born in Wells and went to the Blue Coat School, met mum while he was working at a bakery at King's Stag run by his uncle, Howard Mogg.

When he wasn't baking bloomers, dad could often be found playing the drums in a family dance band which toured the village halls. The star turn was uncle Sid who played the violin while prancing round with the dancers. As Sid was slightly deaf, the farther he moved away from the bandstand, the more difficulty he had keeping time with his fellow musicians. He was unable to hear dad and the rest of them on the stage frantically shouting 'come back here, Sid', and their dances frequently became a shambles, with dad and the rest of the band playing the Last Waltz, and Sid at the back of the hall playing something more akin to a quick step.

We moved to Sherborne soon after I was born, and dad worked as a lorry driver with Western Ways in Bristol Road. The firm was run by Gilbert Ewens, a Dorset county tennis player and a genial chap who always had his employees' interests at heart.

On one occasion he sent a couple of bottles of beer to a driver who had crashed his truck in the countryside. 'I expect Ernie could do with a drink,' said Gilbert, not realising that it was one-too-many which had caused Ernie to mistake a ditch for the road in the first place.

As I grew up in Sherborne, I soon realised that the town represented a microcosm of the country's class system. With a country squire who lived in a castle, and two public schools, it was obvious who pulled the strings in the town.

The Wingfield Digbys not only owned an estate which included a large chunk of Sherborne, but Simon Wingfield Digby was also the Tory MP for that corner of Dorset. A privileged man if ever there was one.

He and his forefathers certainly left their imprint on the town. Their name was everywhere – Digby Road, the Digby Memorial Church Hall, Digby Villas, Lord Digby School (now consigned to the history books), and the Digby Hotel (later converted into a boarding house for Sherborne School). There's even a flagstoned pub called the Digby Tap, although how many times the Wingfield Digby's have popped in there for a pint is open to question.

During my young days the family's power in the town wasn't limited to politics and property. Those who went to the Abbey for Sunday service found another Wingfield Digby, Basil, preaching to them from the pulpit. Strewth, they were everywhere.

In the centre of Sherborne, town was squashed against gown. The main buildings of the boys' public school, together with its open air swimming pool, stood close to the Abbey. The boys' boarding houses were in nearby streets, and the playing fields straddled part of the southern fringe of the town.

During the 1950s Chris Chataway, who went on to be an international middle distance runner and Conservative MP, was a pupil there, as was David Sheppard, who played Test cricket for England before becoming Bishop of Liverpool.

The girls' public school stood on the western edge of Sherborne – far enough away to prevent them meeting up with the boys, or so the headmistress hoped. However, a certain amount of fraternising took place at week-ends when the senior girls were allowed into the town.

Dad was always in a prickly mood when the two schools held their separate commemoration week-ends. The pupils' parents took over the town, the mothers in their Ascot hats and their husbands at the wheels of top-of-the-range cars. 'They've never done an honest day's work in their lives,' he'd mutter.

It's not surprising there was more than a hint of snobbery in the town. Not only did the Wingfield Digby family and the public schools have a big influence on its affairs, but the city and military types who retired there also liked to make their presence felt.

Most of the town's working class had little to do with the 'posh types' and got on with their lives, enjoying their games of skittles and darts. The only time they bristled was when the retired newcomers entered into local controversies. 'They've only been here five minutes and they are trying to tell us how to run the town,' was a common complaint.

In January 1942, however, the town's genteel atmosphere received a jolt when dad and a few like-minded rebels got together and formed the 3/92 branch of the Transport and General Workers' Union in the town.

It was like the second coming of the Tolpuddle Martyrs, although thankfully dad and his band of brothers never faced the threat of being sent to Australia - much to the disappointment of some local employers who would have willingly paid their passage 'down under'.

Among those early pioneers, dad was Branch Secretary, Stan Gale was Chairman, and Tommy Monkton was the branch's secret weapon. He spoke with the rapidity of a machine gun, leaving many an employer bemused and willing to concede to almost any demand.

The branch held its inaugural meeting at The White Hart, and once it got into its stride – it recruited 50 members in next to no time – life was never the same for the bosses of many local companies. They found themselves under constant pressure to improve pay and working conditions, as two branch minute books from the 1940s reveal only too well.

Life wasn't the same, either, for the union's full-time District Secretary, Jack English, who worked from an office at Yeovil. Brother English, who had been enjoying the quiet life hitherto, found himself yearning for some brotherly love as he faced mounting criticism for not dealing quickly enough with problems passed to him by the branch. Dad would often complain: 'He's more on the side of the bosses than he is on ours'. For years I thought his name was Bloody Jack English, which was how dad used to refer to him.

It seems, though, that Brother English got his own back

at one meeting. The minutes for a meeting at the Oddfellows Hall in 1950 record that he gave a 'long and detailed report covering the following matters - new conditions and increase in pay for those employed by British Road Services; Brother Hunt's disablement benefit; case concerning Brother Vickery; matters concerning gas workers, coal distributive trade, hospital workers, government workers and the engineering industry; increase in bus fares and (pause for breath) the case concerning Brother Oakley which was awaiting the decision of the National Trade Group Committee.' As Brother English came to the end of his lengthy report, the sound of snoring could be heard from some parts of the room while other members battled to keep their eyes open.

Tonmore House became the focus of the branch's activities, with a constant stream of members calling to discuss their problems and to use the telephone. In those days few working class families had a phone, so the union branch, after much discussion, had one installed in our flat 'for the use of members'. I don't think any of them used it to phone the bookies, but you never know.

Workers at local firms such as South Western Dairies, the the Marglass glass fibre mills, Seymours bottling plant, Wincanton Transport, Sherborne Council and the Ordnance Depot enrolled as members to help swell the branch numbers.

Bet Dewfall was elected Shop Steward at Wincanton Transport, to become one of the first active women members of the branch.

Dad and his mates, branded as troublemakers by some and admired by others, stuck to their principles and won scores of battles on behalf of local workers. It wasn't too difficult being an active trade unionist in places like

Liverpool during that period, but in Sherborne it took some courage. It certainly cost dad a couple of jobs.

Having such an active Trade Union branch in the town made the local Tories twitchy, and they became twitchier still when the branch held a dance and donated the proceeds of £23.8s.4d to the 'Aid to Russia Fund', at the same time praising the heroic resistance of the Russians in the defence of Stalingrad. Another dance, for the 'Aid to China' fund, raised £7.10s.

Members fighting overseas in the Second World War weren't forgotten either. Six of them each received 50 cigarettes from the branch as a Christmas present in December 1942.

Soon after the war ended, the branch protested at German prisoners-of-war being allowed to drive lorries for the War Agricultural Council in the town when there were local men available to do the job. Fred Stainer, a local builder, was also taken to task for 'dismissing Brother White while continuing to employ Polish labour.' The branch complained to the Disputes Commission, and Mr Stainer was ordered to fire the Polish refugee workers who had settled in Sherborne after fleeing their country during the war.

Talk about a bunch of militants. Dad and his colleagues not only took on local companies, they took on the Union itself in 1949. Their rebellion followed a decision by the Union to bar Communists from holding office. The branch likened it to the McCarthy witchhunt against Communists in America, and dad and the rest of the committee agreed to fight the ban.

The rebels, who included dad, Tom Toy, Ted Oakley, Stan Gale and the rest of the committee, refused to sign the declaration that they weren't Communists. Their defiance led to them being barred from holding office, and the long suffering Jack English found himself having to run the branch from his Yeovil office. They held out until January 1950 when dad announced that, under protest, he had signed the declaration that he was not a Communist. It was all a bit farcical, especially as he was a member of the Communist Party at the time!

Beaten but unbowed, dad went to the Union's national conference that year with a resolution from the branch which told the hierarchy that they wouldn't get any problems from Communists if they 'adopted a more vigorous attitude towards the settlement of disputes and wage claims.'

Knowing that I had ambitions to become a journalist, dad somehow arranged for me to have an interview for a job on the *Daily Worker*'s sports desk. I went to London and was offered the job on the spot. 'But you do understand that you'll be expected to donate ten per cent of your salary towards the paper's running costs,' said the sports editor, a Mr Levenson. I must say the news came as a bit of a surprise, and probably explained why there wasn't a queue of applicants for the job.

It took me only a few seconds to assess that, with so little left in my wage packet, I'd be sleeping underneath the arches with Flanagan and Allen if I took the job. I was keen to become a journalist – but not that keen.

It was one of life's ironies that dad, a lifelong opponent of public schools, should end up living in a town with two of them. It didn't do his blood pressure much good, but it meant that he often hit the headlines with his attacks on public schools at the Union's national conferences.

Reporting on the Union's 1963 conference at Scarborough, *The Daily Herald* gave him star billing under the headline 'Scrap all the public schools'. Describing his speech as the best of the conference, it reported how he had persuaded Britain's largest union to demand a pledge from the Labour Party to close the country's public schools. He told the conference 'this educational privilege should be abolished.'

Not one to mince his words, as I discovered many times during my life, he told another conference: 'Public schools are snob schools, and so long as you have them you will get a steady stream of snobs coming out of them. They should be used as universities.' The public schools withstood his verbal battering, and Wilson's Labour Government ignored his call to scrap them. Dad wasn't surprised.

He always reckoned that the Church was the Tory Party at prayer, and it seemed he had a point on the day the branch celebrated its 21st anniversary with a dinner in the Digby Hall. Attended by the Unions' General Secretary, Frank Cousins, the weather was bitterly cold. The central heating had packed up, and the caterers fought a losing battle to keep the chicken soup and roast turkey hot. As for comedian Nat Kearn and his concert party, they never made it because of the fog and ice. Some of those in the hall were probably quite happy not to have to listen to Sheila Peters, billed as a mezzo soprano of television and radio, but they would probably have enjoyed Len (Uke) Thomas, who rumour had it played the ukulele better than George Formby.

Dad, who proudly told those present that in 21 years the branch membership had grown from 50 to 150, probably made one of the shortest speeches of his career that evening. Afterwards most of those present, including Frank Cousins, wasted no time in making a beeline for the Digby Tap opposite in search of something to warm their spirits.

Later Frank Cousins wrote dad a letter in which he said: 'It was most unfortunate that the unprecedented weather conditions upset some of the plans for your celebrations, but nevertheless I feel the occasion was well worthwhile.'

The branch didn't have the best of luck with its official functions. On another occasion it arranged a dinner at the Half Moon Hotel, only for several of its members to drop out because they had been made redundant and couldn't afford the tickets.

Some were employed by Sherborne Urban District Council which, according to dad's speech at the dinner, had run out of money. He said it was a good job housewives didn't run their homes in the same way, which made him popular with the women present.

In view of dad's political left-wing leanings, it's hardly surprising that my first overseas holiday was to a country behind the Iron Curtain. Myself and a mate, Lawrence 'Jammy' Rowe, spent a fortnight with a lawyer, Boris Stroshack and his family in the small Yugoslavian town of Celje – and very enjoyable it was too, even if we did suffer from aching backsides through sitting on wooden seats for the entire train journey across Europe. Boris, who became a judge in later life, had earlier spent time with us in Sherborne during a study trip.

Dad's trade union and political activities were a spare time occupation, and left little time for anything else. As for mum, she wasn't a political activist, but she devoted hours of her time writing up the minutes of branch meetings, keeping the branch accounts straight, and dealing with queries from members. Her unstinting and uncomplaining support was admired by everyone.

Along with his trade union activities, dad attempted to gain election to Sherborne Urban District Council in 1947 and 1948. He gave it his best shot, but the Tory heartland wasn't impressed by his fiery brand of Socialism, and he was among the also rans both times.

In 1959 the council election was held for the first, and only time, on a Saturday. The experiment was described by *The Western Gazette* as a 'complete failure' with only a 37.8 per cent turn out. The result was announced by the returning officer, Eddie Freeman, at the Long Street schoolroom. Dad – who had stood in the election, again unsuccessfully – told the 100 or so people present that it was a disgrace that so few people had bothered to vote, little realising that in later years anything over 30 per cent would be regarded as a high turnout.

Just like local council elections, General Elections revealed what a dedicated bunch the local Labour Party stalwarts were. Faced with campaigning in one of the safest Conservative seats in the country, both they and the candidate knew they couldn't win, but that didn't stop them fighting a spirited campaign.

Our front room was the campaign headquarters, and leading the charge was Charlie Nash who was known as 'blitz 'em Charlie' because he was always charging into the house on polling day and calling out: 'Our people haven't been voting in Lenthay, we'd better blitz the place.' His rallying cry would lead to an army of canvassers descending on the council estate.

Party activists like Eric Noake – who reputedly once tried to rid his garden of weeds by setting fire to them, but that's another story – Walt Bown and Cyril Davis would knock on doors in the hope of persuading the occupants, who were usually more interested in their herbaceous borders than politics, to get out and vote Labour.

There was no escape for mum, my brother John and I

either. We were roped in to address envelopes, deliver leaflets and, on polling day, keep a check on Labour supporters to ensure they had been to vote. We didn't have a foolproof system, and on election day some Tories were surprised to receive a call from a Labour supporter offering to give them a lift to the polling booth.

During one particularly lively election campaign we woke up to discover that someone had crept up to the front of the house and painted a huge blue 'vote Tory' cross on the pane of glass in the front door. It wasn't long before Charlie Nash came storming up the path saying that the phantom cross painter had called at his house as well. As the morning went by we learned that crosses had been painted on the homes of several other Labour stalwarts.

Revenge was swift. That night two shadowy figures – no, I'm not going to name them – visited the homes of several leading Tories and painted equally large red crosses on the walls. In those days such acts were treated as part of the rough and tumble of local politics, and few if any complained.

With television still in its infancy, eve-of-the-poll election meetings were packed out. I would accompany dad and the Labour clan to the Long Street Schoolroom to heckle Simon Wingfield Digby as he campaigned to retain his Parliamentary seat. Working class meets landed gentry, so to speak.

As a man who was used to his butler and estate workers adopting a deferential air whenever he was around, Wingfield Digby wasn't entirely comfortable at being confronted by his more disrespectful constituents. 'What's your party ever done for the workers?' we'd shout. Or another favourite cry was 'you don't know what you're talking about mate, you don't live in a council house.' It was raucous and generally good humoured, but Wingfield Digby always looked relieved when the time came for him to step down from the stage and retire to the sanctuary of his castle. It was usually the last the man-in-the-street saw of him until he popped up to seek re-election five years later.

The heckling didn't make any difference to the final outcome of the election, but it was great fun and it let him know he wasn't going to have everything his own way. Anyway, his supporters did the same to the Labour candidate, although heckling with public school accents didn't have quite the same impact.

When I say that five years elapsed before we saw Wingfield Digby again, that's not strictly true. He appeared each Boxing Day to hand out a few pennies to any townspeople who cared to wander up to the castle estate yard to receive them. Some saw it as a quaint tradition. Not surprisingly, dad had an alternative view. 'He's still trying to treat people like peasants,' he'd say. 'It's a pity he doesn't pay his estate workers a decent wage.' With that, he put paid to any ideas I might have had of receiving, and spending, one of Simon's pennies.

In those days it wasn't 'Coronation Street' or 'Eastenders' which kept people away from the polling booths - it was the weather. There was a collective groan in our house if we pulled back the curtains on election day and discovered it was raining. It meant the Conservatives had an advantage because they had more cars than us, allowing their supporters to get to the polling booths in the dry, whereas most of ours had to walk.

After gathering at the count to hear the result announced, everyone met at our house for the usual inquest over a glass of whisky. Increasing the Labour candidate's vote by just a handful from the previous General Election was rated a success.

Dad and the rest of them were rarely downhearted, although they were often perplexed at the sight of a 'Vote Conservative' poster in a council house window. 'How can they ever support that lot?' dad would ask.

Towards the end of his life he was in Yeovil hospital recovering from one of his many heart attacks when Margaret Thatcher won the 1979 General Election. He had been a patient there so often that his politics were well known to the staff, so the nurse who told him the Conservatives had won the election, was taken aback when he replied, 'Oh good.'

For a moment she thought his medication had caused a political transformation. 'Mr Mogg, what makes you say that?' she asked, examining his blood to see if it had turned blue.

Dad replied: 'I'm fed up listening to people moan about a Labour government, now they'll get to know what a Tory one is like.' His prediction was more accurate than he imagined.

Dad was the 'red sheep' of a true blue family. His Socialism dated back to the death of his father who was among scores of British soldiers killed in Belgium in the First World War. His mother, like other war widows of the time, received no help from the Government and faced a hard struggle to raise dad and his sister.

Stung by the injustice, he vowed to devote his life to trying to get a fairer deal for the 'common man.' Returning from a union conference in Blackpool by train he wrote that he had looked out at the rows of terraced houses as he passed through Preston, Wigan and Warrington, and hoped that some of the resolutions passed at the conference would 'give the inhabitants of these houses the better conditions they deserve.'

But dad wasn't so serious about politics that he didn't know how to have a good time. On the same piece of paper he described a sing song at the conference that was so 'vociferous' that he almost lost his voice for a couple of days.

Given the nature of the songs, it's safe to assume that Vera Lynn – the forces's sweetheart of the day – wasn't on the platform leading the singing.

I don't think that *The Boss is Having a Terrible Time, Parlez-Vous* is a song which she would have been particularly comfortable with. Dad and his union brothers, on the other hand, loved it.

The first two verses went: *The boss is having a terrible time, parlez-vous (sung twice); Keeping us off the picket line: Hinkey dinkey, parlez-vous.*

'The scabs are having a terrible time, parlez-vous; Getting through the picket line; Hinkey dinkey, parlez vous.'

Another song which raised the roof was *'We Want Nationalisation,'* which had them calling for a national minimum wage in one of the verses. It *only* took about 50 years for their call to be answered.

Sherborne North End football team celebrate a hat-trick of cup wins in one season in the early 1960s. That's me, third from right, holding one of the cups.

The rest of the team are (left to right): Alan Bartlett, Billy Hill, David Manuel, Pete Curtis, Freddy Howe, John Willis, Gerry West (captain), Brian Stainer, Elwin Knobbs and Ernie Male. Missing from the picture is manager Roy Bowles.

The cups were the Yeovil Intermediate League, the Blackmore Vale and the Hayward Memorial.

Frank Cousins (centre), General Secretary of the Transport and General Workers' Union, joins us for a family photo after attending the branch's 21st anniversary dinner in the Church Hall in 1961. With him are (left to right): my mother, me, my father, who was branch secretary for 42 years, and my brother John.

Dad chairs the road haulage rally at Yeovil's Huish Football Ground in 1952. He is flanked by Stan Awbery, Bristol Central Labour MP (sitting with arms folded), and John Peyton, Yeovil's Conservative MP. Addressing the rally is Jack English, the Transport and General Workers' Union district secretary. According to newspaper reports, John Peyton had only a few hecklers to contend with after entering the 'lions' den'.

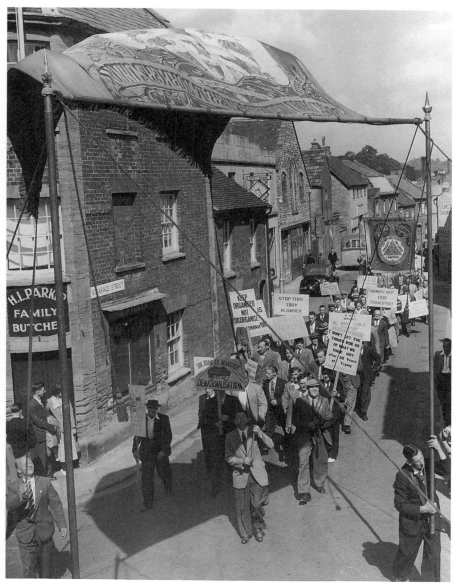

Trade Unionists on the march in Vicarage Street, Yeovil, in 1952, in protest at the Tory Government's plan to de-nationalize the road haulage industry.

Preparing to cycle home after playing tennis on The Terrace. With me are (left to right): Tony Sprague, Terry Chainey and Roy Wilson. The photo was taken by Gordon 'Badger' Guppy in 1954.

7
Teddy Roe

For 364 days of the year Sherborne was like most other country towns, a quiet place where the routine of daily life changed little over the years.

On the 365th day, however, quite a few of the residents seemed to take leave of their senses. They stayed up until midnight and then proceeded to create an almighty racket - all in the name of tradition.

There was nothing remotely musical about Teddy Roe's band, it was simply an excuse to make enough noise to wake everyone up.

It had been taking place for centuries on the first Sunday after October 10th, Old Michaelmas Day, and it was still going strong when I was a youngster.

Anyone could take part, and a large crowd always did. We would meet just before midnight at the bottom of Bristol Road armed with saucepan lids, tin cans with stones inside, football rattles, klaxon horns, whistles and anything else which would create an ear splitting din. One or two musicians brought along their bugles and trumpets, but that was regarded as cheating and they were encouraged to play only flat notes.

Under the watchful eye of the town's bobbies, who were generally not best pleased at having to be on the streets at such an unsociable hour, we set off at the first chime of twelve from the Abbey clock.

To try to ensure some sense of order amid the awful din,

Billy Brown, a local character, led the motley crowd with a lamp held aloft.

At any other time of the year we would have either been arrested or had buckets of water poured over us by bleary eyed residents. But Teddy Roe's band was a tradition for goodness sake, so there were few complaints.

People would get out of bed, look out of the window and cheerfully wave us on our way to the Parade at the bottom of Cheap Street where we dispersed.

No one is certain how Teddy Roe's band started, and to be honest very few of us cared. Some say that the tradition dates back to the completion of the Abbey when the foreman, supposedly called Teddy Roe, celebrated the achievement by leading his craftsmen on a march through the town, banging their tools on the way.

Others say it recalls the days when shepherds brought their sheep to market for Pack Monday Fair. I'll go with the first theory, if only because the ear splitting noise we made would have soon sent sheep disappearing into the night.

Sadly, as the years rolled by, drunken troublemakers latched on to the band and soured what was, in essence, a fun night out.

One year a council official woke up to discover that the contents of his dustbin had been emptied on his lawn, and on another occasion scores of windows were smashed in the Silk Mills factory. The damage was blamed on 'them there louts from Yeovil'.

Each year, as Teddy Roe's Band prepared to set off, the first of the Pack Monday Fair cheapjacks arrived to claim the best pitches on Greenhill and in Cheap Street. Among the regulars was a chap who always wore a straw boater with a hole in the top. His smooth style and gift of the gab enticed the punters to part with their hard earned money for chinaware and other household items. Everyone laughed at his jokes and walked away happy, and he drove off with pockets full of money. It was only when the purchasers arrived home, and opened the boxes, that they discovered they had been palmed off with crockery which was chipped and a load of other junk. If anyone had the last laugh, then it was the man in the straw boater.

Cheapjacks weren't the only spielers who entertained the crowds and relieved them of their money. There were also 'Find the Lady' card sharps and lucky number operators. The numbers were in pieces of drinking straws, and finding a winning one, which allegedly was worth a cash prize, was as difficult as finding the 'lady'.

Entertainers included the Houdini-like escapologist who was handcuffed, chained up and put in a sack. While 'Houdini' wriggled away in the sack, trying to free himself, his partner would warn: 'He's taking much longer than usual to get out. I'm afraid he might be suffocating in there.'

With the onlookers getting concerned, he urged everyone to thrown coins on to the cobblestones in Greenhill where the performance took place. Amazingly, the sound of money hitting the ground always seemed to spur on 'Houdini' to make an extra effort. He would emerge red faced, gasping for breath and free of his chains. His appearance always drew a sigh of relief from the spectators who feared they had been contributing to his funeral costs.

Away from the bustle of the street market, gipsies got down to the serious business of buying and selling horses outside the Antelope Hotel. Onlookers watched from a safe distance as the horses were put through their paces, before a sale was settled with a handshake.

As the day wore on, and the beer flowed, the gipsies

ignored the horses in favour of beating the living daylights out of each other. The police officers usually had the good sense to arrive just as the combatants were staggering away with black eyes and bleeding noses. Oh, and their arms were usually around each other, just to show there were no hard feelings.

Later, the fair behind the Mermaid pub, with its colourful lights and hurdy gurdy music, acted like a magnet. The Anderton and Rowland families would be there with their steam driven rides, including the waltzers and galloping horses, and of course the bumper cars. Later they called them dodgem cars because they wanted to cut their repair bill. Spoilsports – dodging a car wasn't half as much fun as giving it a resounding whack, especially if it was being driven by a girl you had your eye on.

There were swinging boats as well, although I never rode on them because at the back of my mind was the fear that, as the boat swung up into the night sky, I might be pitched out with serious consequences for my health.

I preferred to spend my time visiting both the Wall of Death, where motorcyclists defied the laws of gravity, and Sam McKeown's boxing booth where the legendary Freddie Mills learnt his craft before becoming world cruiserweight champion. Sam would stand on a stage at the front of the booth, microphone in hand, challenging onlookers to take on his group of fearsome looking fighters, whose trademarks were cauliflower ears and squashed noses. 'Step up here anyone who would like to fight one of these professional boxers over three rounds of three minutes each,' said Sam with a voice that seemed to be full of gravel.

Occasionally a local lad, who had lost all sense of discretion after a day's drinking, would strip to the waist, step into the ring and risk his teeth and looks in the cause of entertainment.

Sam's boxers pulled their punches unless they copped one themselves. If that happened, then the local hero usually left the ring with a bleeding nose, water-filled eyes, and a head which was spinning faster than the fairground rides. And all the poor chap could hear, as he vowed never to go within a million miles of Sam McKeown's booth again, was the sound of the crowd laughing its socks off and shouting, 'how many stars can you see now?' His only consolation was that the onlookers usually threw a few bob (called nobbins) into the ring as a thank you for an amusing few minutes.

I was a keen boxing fan in those days. One of my heroes was Bruce Woodock, the Yorkshire coal miner who became British heavyweight champion. I was given a pair of boxing gloves one Christmas, and I rigged up a punch bag in the attic at Tonmore House where I spent hours practising my left jab and right uppercut. But my interest in the sport hit a rapid downward curve when I found myself in the ring at Foster's School against an opponent who promptly knocked me out.

One year in the late 1940s it wasn't just Teddy Roe's Band which woke Sherborne from its slumbers. The arrival of filmakers to make 'The Guinea Pig' also had the town buzzing with excitement. The film, about a working class boy who attends a public school, was made by the Boulting brothers, John and Roy, and starred Richard Attenborough as the boy.

Most of the scenes were shot at Sherborne School and on the playing fields, where boys from Foster's School took part as extras in a cricket match. Everyone looked forward to seeing themselves in the film, but when it was screened their hopes of stardom soon disappeared. They were used only for background shots, and were so far away that even their mothers couldn't recognise them.

The making of the film was a magic time. The executives and stars, who also included Bernard Miles, stayed at the Digby Hotel, and that's where I made for after school to get their autographs. It was the film where Richard Attenborough fell in love with one of the cast, Sheila Sim, whom he later married.

The film also had another claim to fame. These were prim and proper days, so director Roy Boulting must have been delighted when he managed to get the phrase 'kick up the arse' past the censor. His breakthrough captured the headlines and ensured that the 'Guinea Pig' pulled in the audiences.

The 'arse' which was kicked was Richard Attenborough's, and I spent several hours watching the scene being shot in front of the Abbey. His schoolmates put the boot in after making him bow in front of a statue of the fictional school's founder as part of an initiation ceremony.

Like all film-makers, Roy Boulting made Richard do the scene again and again until they were satisfied that his humiliation was painfully realistic. It's a wonder that the kicking didn't end his love affair with films. On the contrary, as we all know, the boot up the backside launched him, almost literally, to a far grander life in showbusiness.

8

Teenage Years

Friday and Saturday evenings during my teenage years were inevitably spent on a pub crawl through the town with a group of mates. A ritual which inevitably left us with light pockets and heavy hangovers.

At the Plume of Feathers in Half Moon Street, Reg the landlord would regail us with the joys of having sex in the sea. A pleasure which, I believe, he had experienced in the Mediterranean rather than in the colder waters of Skegness. Such happy memories seemed to sustain Reg as he stood behind the bar night after night, wondering how on earth he had ended up serving pints of bitter and packets of crisps to the youth of Sherborne.

An apparently well-educated man with a careworn expression, he often said with a weary sigh: 'They say this building has been here for about 300 years, and I feel I've been here for every one of them.'

Clive Church, the licensee at The Britannia round the corner in Westbury, seemed to have no such hang-ups. A retired army colonel, he enjoyed a pint, a cigarette and a gossip. He didn't even object to our rugby-style Saturday evening sing songs. Clive would lean behind the bar and sip a pint with the air of someone who had seen it all before. He probably had – in the officers' mess during his army days.

Another pub, which should perhaps remain nameless, had a licensee with a relaxed attitude to pub life, especially the opening hours. He observed the ritual of calling 'time' on a Friday and Saturday night, but the regulars knew it was simply a signal to carry on drinking in the backroom bar, well away from the prying eyes of the law.

The Wessex Club in Westbury, with Ma Brown behind the bar, had less flexible licensing hours. She pulled down the bar shutter as soon as last orders had been called, but it was a congenial place to meet for all that.

We gravitated to the Wessex Club, which stood opposite the Britannia pub, after becoming too old for the Youth Club. Alongside the bar, which was on the first floor, was a lounge with a snooker table, television set and fruit machine which paid out the occasional jackpot.

Upstairs was the table tennis room where Len Baggs, Terry 'Pongo' Buckler, Pete Tompkins, Terry Henstridge and the rest of us spent many hours practising and playing matches in the Yeovil League.

Rum and orange (a revolting mix, in hindsight) was my tipple in those days. One Saturday evening, however, Mike, one of my drinking mates, invited a few of us into his home to sample his mother's home-made wine. One by one the bottles were opened in the warmth of the front room. 'This one's very nice, what is it?' we asked his mother. 'And this one? It's extremely nice. My goodness, I like this one...' Elderberry wine, crabapple wine, blackberry wine... smooth, and so easy to drink. Too easy to drink, in fact. 'Goodnight,' I said to Mike's mum, giving her a cheery wave. 'Mind how you go,' she replied as we stepped into the cool night air – and immediately found ourselves walking like one-legged sailors in a Force 10 gale. Hound Street seemed to roll from side to side as I searched desperately for a means of support. What happened for the rest of the evening will have to be left to the imagination. I know one thing, it's no good asking me.

My legs tended to be equally uncontrollable during Saturday night dances at the Acreman Street Drill Hall. On the stage was a 10-piece band, and on the floor was me trying to dance the quick step. One... two... three – 'oops, sorry'. One... two... three – 'oops, I'm extremely sorry.' One... two... three – 'oops... Christ, where's she gone?' Ah well, back to the bar.

The cavernous hall – owned by the army – was an unromantic place with its bare lights and even barer walls. The band was perched on a stage made of beer crates, and there were army recruitment posters on the walls. Dressed in our best drain pipe trousered suits, collars and ties, we paid our money at a trestle table before parading across the dance floor.

Watching from the sides were the girls in floral dresses who gazed hopefully at the good looking lads, and gave short shrift to the rest.

Dutch Courage was the order of the day, and we always made a beeline for the bar, a cheerless room alongside the bandstand. If the dance was organised by the Roman Catholics, then the parish priest would sit at one end being plied with drinks by respectful parishioners. 'Would you like another whisky, Father?' He never said 'no', and I never saw him put his hand in his pocket, either, which got me thinking that a life of celibacy did have certain compensations after all.

The wartime influence of American servicemen made itself felt on the dance floor where jiving and jitterbugging were just as popular as the traditional quickstep, waltz and foxtrot. Not that the changes in tempo gained much of a response from some of us. Once out of the bar our dancing was either slow, or extremely slow . . . and slightly unsteady.

The Last Waltz would often be played to a background of insults being traded by one or two hot heads in the car park. It only required one drunk, his tie askew and shirt undone, to say 'who wants a fight, then?', and the night's punch-up would be underway. Fists would fly, noses would bleed, and they would all go home happy.

Apart from the dances, the only other entertainment on offer was at the town's cinema, the Carlton Picture Palace in Newland. There was nothing palatial about the 'palace'. It was a drab place, with wooden floorboards and uncomfortable seats. Outside, posters and black and white photographs, depicting scenes from forthcoming attractions, were displayed in the windows.

Such tear jerkers as the 'Flicka' films, about a horse, and the 'Lassie' films, about a dog, used to pack them in, as did cowboy films featuring Gene Autry and Roy Rogers. Television was in its infancy, and Pathe News, introduced by a cockerel crowing, kept audiences in touch with world events.

Sunday evenings at the Carlton were not for the serious cinema-goer, or for couples wanting to canoodle in the back row, for that matter. It was the night when the local lads piled in for a noisy night out. They liked a really awful film because that gave them an excuse to barrack like a crowd watching a football match. The usherettes, unable to keep any sense of order, sat down and joined in the laughter.

We rarely ventured outside of Sherborne for our entertainment in those early teen years because transport was in short supply. Tony Sprague was the first of my mates to acquire a car, and how we envied him. Boys with a car always pulled the girls. 'She's only going out with him because he's got a car', was a familiar gripe in those days.

Tony did take six of us to Yeovil one evening to see 'Blackboard Jungle', the film which sparked rock and roll mania in this country. Newspapers were full of stories of how city audiences ripped out cinema seats and danced in the aisles as Bill Haley played the film's theme tune 'Rock Around the Clock.'

Nothing like that happened when we watched the film at the Central Cinema. What a civilised lot we were! We contented ourselves with tapping our feet to the music, to the relief of the manager who had been bathed in nervous sweat all through the performance. He could hardly believe that every seat was intact when the curtain came down.

On the journey home we sang, 'One-o-clock . . . two-o-clock . . . three-o-clock . . . rock . . .' – until the engine of Tony's car blew up. The jalopy, which was grossly overloaded, had been emitting worrying creaking sounds throughout the journey and finally gave up the ghost on a particularly steep hill. Tony scrambled out of the driver's seat and watched in horror as steam rose from under the bonnet of his pride and joy.

The Youth Club, housed in the former Macready Rooms, a large stone building in Newland, was the main meeting place for the town's youngsters. The inside of the building was forever being patched up and redecorated in an effort to save it from falling into disrepair.

It was there that a group of us, including Gordon 'Badger' Guppy, Jack Wintersgill and David Wilde, set out to try to persuade the council to provide more teenage entertainment and jobs in the town. We spent several weeks knocking on doors and persuading residents to sign our petition. Our campaign attracted widespread publicity, with coverage on local television, radio stations as well as local papers.

We presented the petition to the town council clerk, Eddie Freeman, who promised to treat our demands with the seriousness they deserved. And that was the last we heard of it. It gathered dust on Eddie's desk until he thought it was safe to put it in the rubbish bin, and that was that. Ah well, it was fun while it lasted.

I suffered similar letdowns when I went rabbiting in the cornfields during the summer months. Looking back, I don't know why I even bothered. Countrywise lads like Robin Northam and Graham Oakley knew exactly when to pounce as the combine harvester cut into the field of corn. They seemed to have telepathic powers, and as soon as the rabbits sped out of the corn they would give them a hefty whack with their sticks. If the rabbits came anywhere near where I was standing they would tiptoe past, safe in the knowledge that I would be too slow to get anywhere near them. Robin and Graham were very generous, however, and usually gave me a couple of rabbits to take home for dinner.

There were quite a few characters in Sherborne in those days, among them 'Tich' Vallard and Bill Gardner. 'Tich', as his nickname suggests, was a cheerful chap who wasn't much taller than the handlebars of the 'high stepper' bicycle he rode. A painter and decorator, he wore a bowler hat and, at a late age, took to playing the drums in a jazz band. He didn't display too much dexterity with the drumsticks, and appeared to tap out more or less the same beat whatever speed his fellow musicians were playing at.

Like 'Tich', Bill Gardner was a true son of Dorset. He had a dry wit and a strong local dialect, as Peter O'Toole found out one day. Bill was standing in a doorway at the bottom of Cheap Street watching the great film actor shooting a scene for 'Goodbye Mr Chips', a musical which was being made in the town.

It was a boiling hot day, and the scene called for O'Toole to run after and jump on a bus as it travelled up Cheap Street. Naturally it was difficult to please the director, and for the umpteenth time he called for the scene to be shot again. As O'Toole came trudging down to the bottom of the street, red faced and perspiring freely, Bill, in his strong Dorset accent, shouted out: 'I bet ee could do wee a drink now, couldnee Peter?' Peter O'Toole, an actor known at that time for his love of the amber nectar, turned round and lifted his right arm in agreement. The impromptu scene sadly wasn't used in the film.

I was in my early teens when we moved from Tonmore House to Vernalls Road – the last road on the right going north out of town – and from there to McCreery Road. The first move was done in the conventional manner, with the furniture in a van. The second move was totally unconventional, with the furniture being carried by me, my brother John, and a few willing helpers.

The decision to dispense with a van was the idea of a muscular neighbour, Jack Coffin. 'You don't need a van, Jack,' he said to dad. 'It's only a five minute walk from here to your new house.' And he was right, that's how long it did take to walk along the allotment path – when you weren't laden down with chairs, tables, bed frames and boxes piled high with our household possessions.

It took me considerably longer than five minutes to do the journey under the weight of an arm chair. My knees buckled half way, with the result that the chair toppled into an allotment, crushing the brussel sprouts and carrots which someone had cultivated with loving care. I was left sprawled in a cabbage patch, much to the amusement of Jack, a giant of a man for whom carrying furniture was a piece of cake. He couldn't understand my difficulties. 'Come on Cliff, we'll never get it done at this rate,' he said as he breezed past, pushing a fridge on a sack truck.

Gasping for breath, I eventually managed to manhandle the chair into our new home, and then promptly collapsed in it. Jack quickly recognised a lost cause when he saw one, and allowed me to carry a few knives and forks after that - with the help of John.

Thanks to that move, we found ourselves living next to Ken and Jean Howard, the best neighbours anyone could have had. Ken and I both enjoyed listening to Ella Fitzgerald, Frank Sinatra and other great jazz singers. Often, when I was in the lounge with the record player on, Ken would hammer on the wall - not to tell me to turn down the volume, but to turn it up so that he could hear the singing better.

Away from the record player (or was it a gramophone in those days?), I followed the Yeo River Jazz Band, with Matto Derrick on clarinet, Geoff Noake (whose dry Dorset humour added to the entertainment) on trombone, Spud Taylor, I believe, on trumpet, Ken Chant on his sousaphone, and on drums Dave Barton, who sold biscuits for a living.

I was a regular at their Friday evening gigs at an hotel in Yeovil, often walking the six miles home to Sherborne in the early hours with their New Orleans numbers ringing in my ears. Sometimes I would travel to London for all-night sessions at Ken Colyer's Jazz club, or to listen to Georgie Fame and the Blue Flames at the Flamingo Club.

Frank Sinatra was one of my heroes. I liked his cool image, with a tilted trilby and loosened tie. I hate to admit it, but I bought a trilby with a jazzy hat band to give myself the Sinatra look, which I used to put on when I listened to his records.

9
Sporting Life

I played most of my football for Sherborne North End in the Yeovil league. We had a lot of fun and won a few cups along the way. Our pitch near the Mermaid was always worth a goal start, especially against those teams with wimpish players who disliked landing in the cow pats when they were tackled. They used to set out on the long journey home stinking of the stuff.

To add to their discomfort our changing room was a wooden hut, a bit like a garden shed, with a few of the wall panels missing. Visiting teams from Yeovil, who were used to the comforts of a brick building to change in, viewed our ramshackle hut with disgust – particularly on those days when the wind and rain whistled through the gaps in the panels and into their nether regions. While we nipped home to a hot bath, they were left shivering and facing a trip back to Yeovil in their sodden kit. Beaten teams caught a cold in more ways than one when they played us in the middle of winter.

Our manager and linesman was Roy Bowles, a painter and decorator who seemed to enjoy the abuse hurled at him by opposing supporters. 'The way you wave that flag, you must be a railway guard,' was one of their politer observations as he waved yet another opposition forward off-side. Roy's liberal interpretation of the off-side law was all well and good until we ventured into some of the neighbouring villages where tough farm labourers were lying in wait.

Roy's flag waving incensed them so much that, at the end of the match when their side had lost, they would chase us out of the field. Somehow, with the angry mob hard on our heels, Roy would melt into the background as we sprinted for our transport. He would wait until the coast was clear before casually reappearing and joining us on the back seat for the journey home. 'What are you all looking so worried about?' he'd ask.

While Roy escaped the wrath of the opposing supporters, it was a different story after the booze ups which accompanied our cup wins. One Boxing Day in particular we celebrated at the Mermaid where the landlord, Theo, filled the cup with a potent mixture of whisky, vodka and any other spirits he had on the top shelf. 'Drink up lads, you deserve this,' he said.

Whatever was in the cup, it tasted good and soon disappeared. Everything appeared to be under control until we walked into the fresh air, and then the world seemed to spin at an alarming rate.

The effects of the potion put paid to the rest of Christmas, and it almost put paid to Roy as our manager. The spirit of seasonal and domestic goodwill vanished as he walked towards his home, treading in the flower beds and stumbling over the doorstep.

But at least he just about managed to stay on his feet, unlike me who went home in a wheelbarrow. Jack Wintersgill, who didn't play for the team but could recognise a player in need, made sure I was comfortable before pushing me along Vernalls Road and depositing me at the front door of my home in McCreery Road. I hoped all would be well as I sang 'God Rest Ye Merry Gentlemen' to the neighbours, but I was wrong. When dad answered the door I sensed that, despite his party hat, his festive mood was distinctly unmerry. I stayed out of sight for the rest of the day... and probably the day after that, although my memory is a trifle hazy as far as that particular period is concerned.

For a short period we had a player, Robin, who needed a few lunchtime pints of cider to perform at his best. It meant we were always fretting whether he would first of all turn up, and then be sober enough to play. To his credit he never let us down, usually arriving just as we were lining up to kick-off. Fuelled by the cider, I'm sure he saw two balls instead of one, which probably accounted for some of his wayward challenges as he stormed around the pitch.

On the other side of the town were our deadly rivals, Sherborne West End, whose manager was Ernie Little. Standing on the touchline wearing his trademark trilby, he didn't have any time for cultured football. Throughout matches his sole instruction to the team was to 'boot it up the field, lads.' He liked to keep the game simple, did Ernie.

But North End and West End were mere minnows compared to Sherborne Town, who in the post war years were captained by Percy Kettle, who had once played professionally. In goal was Ivor Muspratt, and others in that side were Butch Harvey, Ted Chant, Alec Oxford and Les Gallop.

One of the most talented players was a blond-haired youngster called Nicky Payne who attracted the interest of several professional clubs. Word got round one day that they were sending scouts to watch him play, but when they arrived there was no sign of Nicky. He decided he didn't want to put himself in the shop window and, it was claimed, went rabbiting instead.

If we didn't have a match on a Saturday afternoon, then

I would catch the Southern National bus and make for Yeovil Town's ground at Huish where many a 'giant' came a cropper in the FA Cup at the hands of 'The Glovers'.

Everyone seemed to go football crazy on cup days in Yeovil. Shops decked out their windows in the team's colours of green and white, and the match was the only topic of conversation. Walking up Middle Street, wearing a green and white scarf and waving my football rattle, I was a victim of football fever from an early age.

Yeovil's sloping pitch became part of football's folklore, with national newspaper cartoonists depicting players having to use mountaineering equipment to get from one side to the other. It wasn't quite that bad, but it must have seemed like it to the players of mighty Sunderland on that never-to-be forgotten day when Yeovil beat them 2-1 in the FA Cup.

Sunderland were known as the first million pound team, because that is what the players had cost in transfer fees. The team's biggest star was the great Len Shackleton who was a magician with the ball. But he and his team-mates lost their magic touch against Yeovil's heroes led by Alec Stock, the player-manager. They were partly undone by Arthur Hickman, Yeovil's right-back who could kick both the ball and his opponent from Somerset into Dorset if asked. Sunderland's attempt to play cultured football foundered in the face of Arthur's thunderous tackles and agricultural clearances on the small sloping pitch.

Yeovil's famous victory was featured in Pathe News at cinemas throughout the country. Television companies still show the black and white film of that match which put Yeovil into the giantkilling hall of fame. It's been screened so many times it must be stuck together with tape.

Although he was immersed in politics, dad was a football

fan. When I was about 10-years-old he took me to my first big game, Portsmouth versus Arsenal. It should have been a memorable match, instead it was a big letdown. The game was snowed off, so instead of watching Portsmouth's star studded team of those days – which included top internationals Jimmy Dickinson and Jimmy Scoular – we ended up spending the afternoon in a cinema watching Jack Warner in film which had winning the pools as its story line.

Dad more than made up for it later when he took me to London for a holiday and I saw Manchester United play twice in a week, against Chelsea and Charlton. United's goalkeeper Jack Crompton saved a penalty in each of the games, from the great Tommy Lawton at Chelsea, and Don Welsh at Charlton. I've been a United supporter ever since.

Summer months were spent on The Terrace, playing tennis under the blistering sun against the likes of Ken Whitlock, who lived a few doors away in Vernalls Lane and gave me lifts in his 'bubble car', Len Baggs and Clive Church. Clive was the only person I've met whose fitness and stamina seemed to be fuelled by a daily supply of cigarettes and beer.

A shortish man with a beer gut which threatened to burst through his tennis top and shorts, he would refuse to give in as we battled for every point on the red sand-like courts. Our matches lasted for what seemed to be hours, after which Clive would say 'well played old boy' before ambling across The Terrace and back to the Britannia where he was the licensee.

He would leave me – a much younger man – lying on the grass, drenched in sweat and trying desperately to find the strength for the uphill cycle ride home.

By the time I'd arrived home, Clive would already be

hard at work shifting barrels and crates of beer. What a man. He eventually left the Britannia to work as a butler in America where, no doubt, his stamina was put to the test by the constant demands of his tycoon employer.

The groundsman at The Terrace was Bill Bailey, a tall weather-beaten man who brought a certain military precision to his work. He spent hours keeping the ground immaculate – and it broke his heart to see sportsmen ruining his handiwork. He would watch stony-faced as cricketers dug their bats into the beautifully prepared square, and tennis players skidded across the pristine shale tennis courts which he had spent hours watering and rolling.

Bill realised he had to suffer in silence as far as we sportsmen were concerned, but woe betide casual visitors who stepped out of line. Bill kept watch on his domain with radar-like eyesight. He would be nowhere to be seen until, say, a parent stepped on to the cricket square to retrieve his youngster's ball. Then Bill, his face like thunder, would come striding across The Terrace to give the embarrassed culprit a right old dressing down. He would then spend the next fifteen minutes putting the blades of grass back in place on his piece of hallowed turf.

10

Reluctant Apprentice

On leaving school I wanted to be a newspaper reporter, but compromised under parental pressure and became an apprentice printer instead. 'Journalism is a risky business,' dad said. 'You ought to learn a trade first.' The following five years at *The Western Gazette* were interesting, but not always rewarding.

For a start the composing room on the top floor of Sherborne Road office was hot, noisy and claustrophobic - not the place for someone who likes the great outdoors. The heat and noise was created by a battery of linotype machines which turned molten metal into 'slugs' of type which made up the newspaper's printed pages.

The Linotype operator spent hour after hour tapping away at the keyboard while squinting at reporters' hand or typewritten stories. I soon decided that, whatever straitened circumstances lay ahead of me, it was the one job I would never do. Not only did it seem to be a tedious way to earn a living, but I didn't want to develop a permanent squint either.

We worked long hours, with Wednesday, when that week's paper was 'put to bed', being the killer day. We were there from eight in the morning until nine at night, and possibly longer if the older printers managed to string out their tasks for an extra hour's overtime.

Thankfully there was always plenty of banter in the composing room – provided the foreman, Harry Cox, wasn't around. He might have smiled once while I was there, but I can't swear to it. Immaculately dressed in a blue pinstripe suit, with waistcoat, he regularly patrolled the newsroom to make sure everyone was at work.

He didn't indulge in idle chit chat, and he certainly didn't crack any jokes. If the sound of laughter rose above the clatter of the linotype machines, he would stride through the newsroom, hands behind his back, towards the source of the merriment and fix those involved with his icy stare.

To be fair, Harry had the onerous job of making sure *The Western Gazette* and two others, *Pulman's Weekly News* and a Taunton paper, were published on time each week. He seemed to think (not without some foundation) that I wasn't totally supporting him in this objective.

We didn't get on too well, Harry and I. He was forever coming up to me and saying 'Clifford, can I have a word with you?' After we entered his glass panelled office, which gave him a view of most of the composing room, he would usually begin 'I'm not too happy with the way you...' Then would follow the inevitable dressing down, which usually washed over me because I'd heard it many times before.

He became particularly tetchy if he caught me looking wistfully out of the window for thirty seconds, and woe betide any of us if we were so much as a couple of minutes late for work.

As we ran up the iron staircase and in through the door, Harry would be standing outside his office, grim faced, making sure that we were fully aware that the timekeeping lapse had been noted. Sometimes I tried to sneak in through the front entrance, but it was always to no avail. The fact that I wasn't wearing my grey smock was the giveaway, and my name inevitably went into his black book.

Despite Harry's best endeavours he never established total control over his workforce. Oliver Collins, a senior printer who enjoyed a regular pinch of snuff and a sneeze, was one who had acquired the knack of gossiping without being caught.

Oliver always seemed to have a cataclysmic week-end, and the first hour of each Monday would be spent recounting his latest brush with disaster. Wiping his nose with a snuff stained handkerchief, his opening words would be 'Eer, you'd never believe what happened to me...'. Walking into plate-glass shop doors, dropping hammers on his feet, falling off his bike, toppling out of trees – Oliver's week-ends were a tale of one mishap after another. How he survived I'll never know.

Due to an accident of birth his head was permanently tilted slightly to the right, and this seemed to help him to see round corners as he moved from one linotype operator to the other with his tales of woe. Consequently he was able to stay one step ahead of Harry – and he always did. Sometimes Harry would be alerted by the sound of Oliver sneezing uncontrollably, and blowing his snuff-filled nose in a far corner of the room. But by the time he got there Oliver was nowhere to be seen.

Leg pulling was part of the composing room culture, and the principal victim was a linotype operator called Wilf. He was picked on because he had a low sense-of-humour threshold. Or to put it another way, he always blew his top after discovering that he had been picked on yet again.

One day he arrived for work proudly wearing a new overcoat. As he prepared to leave for lunch, someone managed to fix to the back of his coat a sheet of paper with 'sale item' written on it in large letters. Wilf walked home unaware of the puzzled looks he was attracting from other pedestrians. Naturally he saw the piece of paper when he got indoors. With his stress levels rising, his lunch remained

uneaten and he was soon beating a furious path back to the
Gazette. It's best to draw a veil over the scene in the
composing room as we greeted him with 'you're back early,
Wilf. You'll get indigestion if you eat your food that
quickly...'. Childish humour, perhaps, but it was irresistible
given Wilf's apoplectic reactions.

Near the newsroom were the readers whose job it was to
check the galley proofs of type for mistakes. The proofs
were sent back to the linotype operators to be corrected,
and then they were read again to ensure no mistakes had
slipped through.

The head reader was Mr Hamblin, who was a stickler for
accuracy. He and his right-hand man, Mr Brook, kept a
close eye on the half dozen or so women who worked in
pairs, one reading the original copy and the other marking
the proofs. As press day approached, and the pressure
mounted, the room had the sound of humming bees as they
read quietly and at speed.

On the floor below the sub-editors knocked the copy into
shape, correcting factual errors and keeping a keen eye
open for any libels which, if they slipped through, could
have cost the paper a pretty penny.

The *Gazette* was a family affair at that time. Mr
Hamblin's daughter worked alongside him, one of the sub-
editors was Wally Elliott, son of the managing director, and
working in the newsroom were the Martin brothers, as well
as Doug Kendall and Ron Ostler (related by marriage),
Oliver Tompkins and his son, and a linotype operator
named Pryor whose son, David, joined as a reporter and
later became the editor.

As much as I disliked working in the newsroom, the job
did have one benefit. It gave me an insight into the world of
journalism. I started contributing news and sports stories to

the paper, and ended up writing regular football reports.

Sherborne North End, the team I played for, featured regularly in these reports. I soon cottoned on to what is meant by 'journalistic licence', so that our victories were usually described as 'magnificent', and our defeats as 'unlucky'. Modesty should have prevented me from ever mentioning myself, but it didn't! According to those reports I scored some amazing goals.

Eric Pike, a sub-editor and former Sherborne district reporter, gave me great encouragement, and Don Mildenhall, who took his place in Sherborne, became used to me knocking on the door of his home in McCreery Road with my latest piece of news copy.

The editor, John Goodchild, was a giant of a man, but a remote figure as far as I was concerned. Among the reporters was David Foot who went on to become a cricket writer for the *Guardian* and author of several books on the sport.

Despite many shaky moments – which even included a threat of the sack from the *Gazette*'s managing director, Daniel Elliott – I completed (or should it be 'survived') my five-year apprenticeship.

As I left on my final day Harry Cox sighed with relief, and I let out a loud 'whoopee' as I hung up my smock and strode out of the newsroom for the last time.

Towards the end of my time at the *Gazette* I received my National Service call-up papers. I wasn't overjoyed at the prospect of spending two years' in uniform, and decided that I'd have a stab at failing the medical.

My Uncle Nett's flat feet were enough to keep him in civvy street, so I studied how he walked before reporting to a services' medic in Salisbury for my examination. 'Take your shoes and socks off, Mogg, and walk across the room,' ordered the purple faced old doctor. So off I went, feet splayed as wide as I could get them, waddling like a duck. 'Walk back again,' ordered the doctor. By now my ankles were aching and my waddle had become a hobble. 'Excellent,' said the doctor who, as far as I could see, would have given the OK to a man with a wooden leg.

'Now drop your trousers,' he said. The game was up. I stood upright in front of him, my trousers and pants round my ankles. The doctor gazed at my testicles with the bored look of someone for whom the sight of private parts had long since lost its novelty value. 'Cough,' he said. 'And again.' Hey, he's seen something which isn't quite right, I thought. Maybe he's going to show me the door after all. 'Cough again, Mogg,' he said a third time. So I did, screwing up my eyes as though the slightest cough was causing me an excruciating pain down below. 'Excellent,' he said again.

So that was it. One short walk and three coughs, together with a quick check of my heartbeat, and I was judged fit enough to withstand the rigours of service life. Like scores of other young men of my age group, I would be spending the next two years defending the country.

To say I defended the country is stretching it a bit. As 5049880 SAC Mogg, I landed a cushy office job with the RAF in the Lincolnshire countryside, where I succumed to hay fever through too much sun bathing. I've suffered from it ever since.